Amelie

Amelie never forgot the first time she saw an Aurora Borealis, It was truly magical, she saw through the crystal windows as her eyes truly opened to the overflowing silvery light, atoms aligned with her molecules, that are the stars, the home of her spirit, that breathes the cosmos, she was a starchild, her eyes shone like diamond, dark that unveils the light within, the light of the true love, that is eternally the end and beginning, as her Ugg boots softly touched the snow, and she looked the white mist, and saw her cottage in the distance, as she layed in her bed and changed to her cream coloured night gown, she lay in her soft, warm bed with wool cover as slept.

Her spirit then wandered into the sea of dreams, where she saw her lover in the distance, and thought, "I miss how you touch my soul and we passionately swim into a thousand layers of exploration of our luminescent souls, I miss your eyes, their warmth, one glance opens the wings of my soul, and thus, as you gaze into me, we become the wind that floats upon our naked spirits" as so, their souls become the wind that floated upon their naked spirits, they became the water in the sea of gold, where their spirits swam in the deep waters, and their presences flow over each other as they aimlessly swayed at the regions where sound never reaches, where only the true music of their souls chants the light that touches the slow dance in the sun of her lover's aura, her heart rushes and glows gold as they kiss, ripples of heaven, angelic breath in the sea. Amelie believed in true love, she believed in the true love achieved through meditation, the beautiful clarity she felt as she walked upon the water, as she walked, the wind began to stream through her ears, she heard the wisdom that told her, you are the water, earth, wind, and fire. The wind then flew her over the forests, the wind then began to make the leaves dance like winged, delicate butterflies, fluttering, like the leaves on the thousands of those leaves on the thousands of trees, those leaves shook and made an orchestral sound, music to the soul. As she rose above the atmosphere, before her feet touched a sea of clarity, touched with the white petals of lotus, she saw his soul near to her soul, their hands touched, they kissed and their their stars became one.

Beach

Dawn reflects a sea of stars as she walked by the beach in Biarritz, she noticed a solitary, handsome young frenchman reading "Rimas" by Gustavo Adolfo Becquer, she greeted him and after they talked awhile, she said "I love that book, It's one of my favorites" as she lay down next to him, "you know my name is Juliet, and that i come as a tourist from London, Britain, tell me, Jean-Luc, what part of France do you come from?" he then replied, "I come from Le Grau De Roi, but i frequently like to wander and visit Biarritz. I have not finished the entire book Juliet, is it good? is it beautiful?" "the book? It is a true gem, it's poetry is like a magnifying glass. It brings to life the full vividity of the painted imagery, that shines the true meaning under a light, poetry, i believe is a beautiful language that illuminates the altar of the soul, do you love the sea, Jean-Luc? do you believe that it is beautiful" "it is..." as Jean-Luc tousles Juliet's soft, dark locks, "I believe, Juliet, that beauty shines through the altered consciousness, nature is a blending of poetry and grace, beauty arrests space and time, and allows the soul to be lost in the slow dance, in which the tree leaves sway to the hazy glow of the sun". They then arose from the beach sands and began to walk with their bare feet, holding shoes in hands, as the lush, soft haired water nymphs, Oceanids, that were silken through the clear ocean water, while the Asteriae glowed in the celestial heavens, Juliet was born in the cosmos and raised in the dew of starlight, she came from the violet painted in a midnight dream, a traveller of space and time, in the night sea, the stars tessellate with the her eyes, windows to her soul that saw the light upon the calmness of the human shore, she closed her eyes as she was surrounded, the water became her, the secret garden of the stars.

"Juliet?" "yes, Jean-Luc?" "whenever i hear the waves crashing on the shore, I like to think that they resound the hymn of the universe that heralds a rising dawn in the night of the soul, shadows that fade to light shimmer upon those waves that crash through my soul, you asked me before if i loved the sea. I do, so much, that i faded into the waters of your sea, in the glow of your light, i am a silhouette immersed in the deep waters of your eyes. I feel somehow relaxed, comfortably numb in the eternal silence of your sea that breathes the light of stars alive, within dreams of you, whispered into the depths of my soul, with you, i sway in the sea of the infinite, where heaven glows within us, we are divinity."

And so they walked back into the cottage illuminated by colourful glass lamps, "love is infinite", Juliet whispered as they sat on the balcony couch, watching the stars trailblaze across the night sky, flowing light years.

Beautiful Minds

Her coffee cup touched the wooden, oak table as she told her lover, "William, i wish that we could have more time to speak to each other more". He then replies "sometimes, Sophie, constantly speaking to one another does not necessarily mean true communication" "but what is true communication, William?" "true communication, Sophie, is the language of the heart", he then continued, "when lips move, nothing happens, when hearts speak, seasons are born, as the eyes shine like a sea of diamonds in the night, darkness unveils light, the light that is love, which is, a beautiful spirit of higher wisdom and knowledge, gentle like white wings of a dove, in the night ocean.

After a few hours, William said: "My dear Sophie, let us move away from this cafe, and into the surrounding large gardens". And so they arose from their seats after paying the bill, and then walked into the endless, lush, green gardens in which the cafe had sheltered itself, as they walked for a good hour, William began to speak again, "is it not better, Sophie, that we are talking in a voyage through which we immerse ourselves into the stars, that move against the sky like a wave, that moves in sleep?"

"can you tell me more about sleep, William?"

"sleep is the night veil of infinity, my dear Sophie"

"but should we not wake up?" Sophie asked

"what would we wake up from, Sophie? life itself is a dream, and we are its subjects"

"subjects?" she inquired

"yes, Sophie, subjects like this universe and its components, we are made of the matter, the matter in which we were created by God, and that purity, we shall return to when our time has come to pass away"

"Sophie, how would you compare an ideal human to a tree?"

"Perhaps, William, the ideal human, would be strong, and supportive, and resistant to the destruction of humanity through the corruption ax, and yet, be generous enough to let the leaves of kindness grow through the branches of his heart, and the tree will bloom flowers of prosperity. The tree, which is like the human, with the balance of its leaves and its bark, will form a balance through which inner peace is achieved".

"And when humans achieve inner peace, that peace will spread like roots through the earth, growing influence, birthing trees until the barren earth is a lush, green Garden Of Eden."

Sophie and William walked up a green, moss lined path towards the river, their steps were gently lit by the sun.

"Sophie.."

"Yes, my dear?"

"I feel quite impatient"

"Why do you feel impatient? patience is an important value, the gardener is patient that the bud will bloom into the flower, however, the gardener is also patient with the streams of life, that the flower will face strong winds, hurricanes, as it will also embrace the nourishing power of sun and water. Patience is when the ocean knows that will face strong winds, and, if patience is not maintained, those strong winds will cause tsunamis, and chaos, now, there is the exception of when chaos can be used to topple down dictators, oppressive regimes, and inward totalitarianism. However, from chaos, corruption can rise as well, for the world is not black and white, it will always be, many shades of grey".

"I wholly agree, dear Sophie, i see that we have reached a river, let us sit down by this fig tree"

And so Sophie and William sat close together by a beautiful, big and grand fig tree, Sophie, with the support of William, who was 6 feet tall, she had plucked the plump and juicy figs and placed them in her bag, "Are you sure you can do this, Sophie?" "The owner of the gardens is a very good friend of mine and has given me permission to pluck only from this tree"

Williams lowers Sophie as she then places a large clay bowl on the soil and rinsed the white figs with the cool water from her bottle, scrubbing the dirt off gently with her small fingers, that twist off the stems, before finally gently drying them with paper towels, she peeled the skin away starting from the exposed top, the figs were ripe, so they could sometimes ooze a sugary syrup, that crystallizes on the surface like diamonds, she takes one into her mouth and bites it, the explosion of freshness and sweetness illuminated her tastebuds, at that moment, she felt very much, and truly alive. She then continued with the other figs and shared the precious fruits with William.

As they sat down by the river, as the gentle light from the sky touches every leaf, as Sophie and William had glown with them, "the sun..." Sophie whispered, William raises his head from her shoulder, "did you say something, Sophie?" "the sun, it shines on our skin, the transparent calligraphy of love."

William and Sophie then witness two butterflies flying close together, dancing and twirling, Sophie then began to speak "how could nature be so delicate and powerful like butterflies?" "like yin and yang, the world is at balance, fish and water, grass and soil, dew of rain, raining of dew on river and how it flows with other rivers towards the ocean, how the dandelions are carried by the gentle wind that currently caresses my own face, the face of my soul, William, physically, i am a human, emotionally, i am high-flying, high-soaring bird of light"

The birds gently chirp in the background, "they are full of love like us, William, their love blends with the melody of their souls, these trees hang its clear lanterns..."

"Clear lanterns? Sophie, but i see no clear lanterns in these trees"

"The lanterns are the leaves, flowers and fruits of the trees, and their light of their cells and particles are glowing clear, William, for to see clearly is poetry, everything you see is created by God."

A deep silence then revives the listening of Sophie and William, by the riverbank, like the ground blossoming green in a spring wind, like the melody of the growing being inside the egg, like this universe coming into existence, the lovers, William and Sophie, awaken and emotionally praise with their hearts, love spreads through the gardens of the soul.

William then speaks, "Sophie, look at the sky, what do you see?"

"I see the sun, the blue sky, and a cloud that is shaped like a flower"

"Look deeper, Sophie" as their fingers entertwined and their hands were held closely.

Sophie then contemplated for a few minutes, and said to her lover,

"In the sun, I see the center, liquid fire through which organisms like us swim, swimming through many layers, layers of the sky ocean through which blooms the flower from the water, I carry that flower and also the star that blooms from the night veil because i know that they are a part of me. I am like the flower that glows from the soil, and reborn as the stars circulate the earth, how fish flows in the ocean of light, the sun aligns with the moon in twilight, lovers, like us, unite and their souls become one, their hands touch the earth, eternal, like their own beautiful minds."

Canoe

Heavy headed and weary of the shadows of realism, i entered the soft bed of love, nestled in the spiritual, all encompassing light of God, healing my wounds, as i, like a soft gentle child of the stars, gentle blanket dissolving from my body, and into the traveling canoe, where i swam in the milky sea of clouds, as my clarity and peace illuminates, my lotus flower blooms as my white dress flows in the wind that gently caresses my canoe into the heavens, immersed in the surrounding light, we are one with the stars, lovers in the canoe flowing in the endless sea of space, deep field, into the unknown, to be honest, i have given way too much of my time to what we call the real world, let start living for our dreams, lets start embracing the true love within us and spread it to the world and give it to the world, let us be marine mammals in the sea of love, let us become non physical and immerse in meditation, peace, and prayer, spreading love until humanity is one family again.

We must have peace, because bombs explode through houses, flames explode on the t.v screen, the pure terror on my face of seeing politicians and their angry faces on the screen as innocent civilians run from burning homes, the innocent are strangers in the foreign field of war, their spirits floating from the cruel, bloodied blade of corrupt dictators and politicians and from the ashes of war. From the darkness of a storm, will come the light of hope.

I thought those ideas as i rowed my canoe in a galactic odyssey, the waves break and the paradise of love invites, so let it in, and the healing will begin.

Elizabeth

Elizabeth was a lonely girl, a shy female who loved to be in the library, she read classics like "Pride and Prejudice", "Jane Eyre", and even "Wuthering Heights" even though she cried at the end of it. Elizabeth felt like no one understood her deep, passionate love for detail and the small, beautiful things like the delicate veins on leaves that vine like the different life paths of each individual being, water flowing through the veins of the leaves and the anatomy of the human, Elizabeth had deeply loved poetry, almost to the degree where she sank into the passionate fury of its bonfire arms, warmth through the mist of her spirit, flaming words dancing like leaves, inferno glowing through her eyes as she currently embraced a page of the book "The Waves" by Virginia Woolf. She sat down in a quiet corner in the library and continued to read, her spirit delving through a thousand layers of waves, the sun sets upon the physical world, an ocean of light washes over Elizabeth's shore, calmness settles, the spirits of clouds rise through her current mind of clarity, as Elizabeth continues to read, quiet images of breath merge with the waters of consciousness.

Elizabeth was a little white dandelion that everyone looked past, every day, the dandelion grew more beautiful and strong from the concrete, and yet, everyone still walked past the dandelion, and into the clouds, clouds in the minds of humanity that walked upon the water, that possesses a thousand centuries, mysteries of cosmos, as the humans that walked past the dandelions became the clouds, the dandelion begins to grow, It's florets bloom, one may suddenly notice the dandelion, and so, the flowers of enlightenment bloom from human to human until, there is an eternal heaven within humanity, a kingdom of skies.

Elizabeth felt alive in the presence of nature, in the robes of an angel of light as she imagines herself walking through the lavender fields, smelling the lavenders, feel their calming sensation on the breathe of her spirit, as she lays her head down in the softness of the clouds, that bring fresh showers for the flowers, the leaves of a flower gently shake as a butterfly flutters it's wings into the sky, over earth and ocean, in gentle motion, light fades to shade, the butterfly floats over the depths of the purple sea through the midnight breezes strewn, the moon illuminates it's aura of pearl, light fills the vapour of mist, as the aerial hue of roses fill the water, her soul was an enchanted boat that floated upon the silver waves of dreams, the waves sing like angels with all the winds of melody ringing, the waves of dreams seem to float forever over the ocean, in which her soul floats into the sea, where the winds and the waves stream through the harmonization of love.

Elizabeth attempted to reach out in the social world, but she was embraced with rejection, the sad, lonely flower in the barren field, petals blooming through the secrets of the similar, lonely hearts becoming one with the vines of the earth. Elizabeth truly, and deeply loves nature, she loves the odours and colours of roses, all of their elements, blossoming systems of thought in mist of her garden of wisdom. As she walked through the hallways of the library, she thought of how the true wisdom was found in the poets that write with the breathings of the spirits that colour with the evanescent hues of the ethereal world, a painting of a scene or passion, touching the enchanted chord, ascending light and fire from the shadows of the mind, arresting the vanishing apparitions of thoughts, veiling them in language, Elizabeth knew that poetry is a portal of the expression of interpenetration of a diviner nature of the human that transmutes all that it touches, the radiance of the human's presence is wreathed in the incarnation of the spirit which breathes the fragance of love. Elizabeth thought of the subject of love, is love what the flowers feel for the sun? what the sun feels for the leaves? their dew drops inclastendine through the innocence in the eyes of a child? the unconditional love felt for the mother? she contemplated that the eyes are gems within the superclusters, clusters of words, cause and human reaction, emotion and its different coloured silks, the rose is blooming in twilight, the stars as the sun arises in the eyes of the human, whose love, in all of its forms, does not know boundary.

Elizabeth sat at the library table with a few strangers, she began to think that the bird never hesitates to leave it's cage, and so the human must never hesitate to leave his/her psychological, emotional cage, though sometimes, she thought that maybe the humanity was living under a psychological cage and needs to know that we, in the universe, are not alone.

Even though, Elizabeth began to contemplate, she, as a human, is alone, she is everyone. She believed that the veins of humanity are wreathed with particles of man and woman, veiled by the waves of life, that crash upon the shores of Infinity.

She then walked out of the library and drove through the streets, the car was illuminated by the white light of the sea of stars, that was her true home.

Elizabeth then reached the doorsteps of her human home, she was met by her white persian cat, blue eyes shining, her white paws padded at her feet, before climbing to her shoulder, Elizabeth held her close, soft cashmere fur warm against her skin.

Elizabeth, in the morning that arose from the warmth of night, had decided to drive to the park,

She then opened her eyes, her spirit had called her to explore, she arose and found a white rose, though, rather than fully contemplating the rose, she explored it's components that made its perfection, symmetric to how the veins, heart and other structures make the human anatomy. Touching the surface of the leaf, she contemplated simple it was, and yet, how beautifully it balanced the universe.

She then left the rose and drove to the Australian embassy to get her passport after her excessive imagination about the beach, time passes and she achieves her passport, on the airplane, she slept for quite a while until she was refreshed and saw the view from her window.

Reader, it was magnificent, the airplane wings had flown through the rising kingdom of skies, through which the milky seas had streamed through the golden glow of heaven.

In her mind, she began to praise the view and say light, glimmer through the ocean between the butterfly and the petal, the moon and the sheets of diamonds in the eyes of human that has dispersed into the ocean of pure serenity.

The airplane gently lands from the kingdom to the earth, heat of friction igniting the wheels like the hooves of wild horses against the ground. After finishing airport legal processes and collecting her baggage, she then drove to the hotel and relaxed in bed, at the time Elizabeth had arrived, the sun was setting, and so, she called the sun to rise, to rise from the shadows and let the lion of the heart roar through embers of eyes, that flame in the trails of unknown, burning through the stars, igniting the night ocean alive. She closed her eyes, as her spirit became one with the stars.

The sun finally rose, as her spirit returns to her body, she arose to have breakfast and walked down to beach, which was shining and beautiful, far more beautiful than any other beach in the world, she sat in a chair with a container of lemonade, as she drank the lemonade, she closed her eyes and felt the feeling of freshness of the salty ocean spray against her crisp white dress, cold lemonade sugar on her tastebuds, sweetness energizes her legs that launch her from the chair and into the air, white dress flying, she was the spirit of euphoria. She then opened her eyes, and saw the ocean, and how the seabirds trail against the waves of light.

Endless Love

Her spirit dances through a veiled mist, in the warm glow, she felt his essence, wafting smells awaken her senses, bare feet wanderlust in the mist of passion, roses surrounding my body, their scent rich and sweet, veiling my heart. I am a fool to want him, to love him, i looked in the mirror, who was i? i was numb, the mirror reflects the clarity of my eyes, yet my heart was blind, different faces of my life, reflections in the mirror change, i had seen and felt the presence of beautiful souls and became them, as they became me, for our souls are one and the same, except, my soul felt his soul glow warmth through his whispered words touching my heart, the listener within the eyes that flows the water flooding as my body is rushed into the crashing and overwhelming waves pushed by the wind. In the wild waters, i only heard my heart beating, rushing, holding my palms to my heart to protect it, as the water slows and i sleep in bed, every night, haunting, beautiful dreams of the paradise within my flower that blooms when i am bathed in the light of his heaven. As you caress my skin and he feels through the depths of my soul, i knew he could never be mine, as the red silk of desire slips on my skin, roses bloom in an endless vivid dream, flames of passion in the depths of endless love.

Freyr

11th century: Norway

I woke up 2 hours before 7:00 am to eat my *Dagmal*, or day meal, before the fire of the norse god of sun "*Sol*" burned through my fingertips as I labored 24 hours everyday for the rest of my life as an *Ambatt* heaving myself from the wooden platform bed. I headed out of the *Longhouse*, or a straw covered cottage with oak wood walls, as I walked through the lush green grass to the storehouse, the weather in Skjolden was baltic, but it was at the end of the Sognefjord, the longest fjord in Sognefjord, Norway so it offered a bounty of herring and salmon. As I headed to the *byre*, I grabbed a small portion of crabapple berries, a bag of oats for *grautr* and a hunk of beef, I stoked the fire at the *Maledr* as I hanged the chain and boiled the beef in a iron cauldron, after fishing it out by using an iron hook, I cooked the oats with water in the cauldron when Rögnveig Guilhoff, the 10 year only child of the jarl Bjorg Guilhoff and his wife Brunnhildr, ran to me and hugged me. They have left him entirely to my caretaking job as a nanny, "Good morning, the *gull* of your hair shines in all of its *vegr*, but, why did you have to chop it?" "thank you, Rögnveig, but as an *Ambatt,* or *Thrall,* which is the male version of my place as *serf*, men and women alike must chop their hair to show their servitude." My dark brown eyes were suddenly shrouded in deep tears, he stood there silently until I wiped them with my hands, and he asked me when was his father coming back, so i told him he will be back on *thorsdagr*, after offering him a bowl of grautr before he walked away.

The sad, real truth was the fact that his father, the Jarl Rognar Guillhoff was out emptying the *Horn*, while the hours of my days were spent under the burning sun churning the butter, and preparing the goat's and cow's *Mjolka* and heaving the sacks to preserve the food for preservation through *Vetr,* and back-breaking tasks of grinding corn and salt using using the rotary hand quern, in addition to many other duties, while she would nothing but sit at the loom and weave.

When I returned to the longhouse, Brunhildr, the mother of the family, was preparing *Dyresteg* which is reindeer meat with norwegian goat cheese sauce and *Lefse* which is norwegian potato pancakes, she was wearing her *Hangerock* which is an apron skirt and flowing, luminous linen white headdress that spread over her back that swayed to face me when I entered, heaving the baskets of fruit and vegetables, she was looking over my own plain, undyed tunic and slave collar still tightly bound to my fate, I felt her youth even though we were the same age, which was around 27.

"I need you to *mjolka* the cows and use the rotary hand quern today, the bread and milk quantity is drying out, take care of the *dyre* and clean the poop, and wash the familys clothes, especially Rognar's, he is returning from successful raids and plunder today and expects a feast, we will prepare hefty amounts of *bjorr*..." seeing my distressed face, she darkly smiles and says "need not for you to worry, *serf,* I will do by best to not let him drink too much and will take him to his bed early, now go."

The night of the *Nattmal* feast came at the eternal riding of *Mani* on her chariot, Rognar Guillhoff came thundering in, Rögnveig came rushing in and Rognar held him tight in his arms, "my son!" breathing out a thousand interlockings in his war-ridden chest and by the norse gods, blessing his son , by giving a final kiss on his cheek, he dropped his son and embraced his wife, and, before he left to unpack, he intensely whispered in my ear, "I wish to help you escape Norway, you will not endure this any longer."

The whole family sat down outside at a oak wooden table, Brunnhild had deceived me, she started to boast and to seduce Rognar, pushing him to drink more, he then requested me to his presence near the stable, we met there and he stated: "You might that Brunnhilde is a good person, but I know she despises you and wants to cruelly torture you, but I have never been weak, you will take the white mare and escape this home." Rognar places in my hands a bag of fruits and vegetables, biscuit bread and, to my slight delight, an amphorae of water, and *hvönn* which was a healing herb that is related to Eir, the norse healing goddess, he had also given me his fur coat, " I bid you on your way, my lady" Rognar says and kisses my hand.

And so I begin my long journey,

 I take the sturdiest white mare and rode 10 *Akrlengds* out of Rognars lands, when I finally stopped after 2 hours, I let my horse graze while I rested under a tree, I began to sew my heartstrings onto the fabric, sewing the glory of a part of Asgards paradise, I drew intricate knots and vining flowers when my time shredded it out. My eyes began to overflow with tears as I remember when I was separated from my mother and father at the slave market, the Viking raiders brought us from our hometown,they would pick different slaves according to their strength and stability, they ever so firmly held my hand and told me to be strong, hugging me tightly, their warmth stayed in my heart. After many hours, I had grown tired and fell into the depth of sleep.

I woke up under the golden talons of a large white falcon, my mind was still too groggy to ask where I was going, where it was taking me, I only smiled because I was freed from slavery. The falcons feathers started to beat faster until it reached the speed of sound, gripping its talons tighter to my thin body, I felt my skin clinging to my bones.

11 century: Asgard

The falcon rose above Earth's atmosphere and onto the *Bilröst* bridge, it flew above the burning luminous rainbow and reached *Himinbjörg*, or heavens castle, which is the dwelling of *Heimdallr*, the watchkeeper of the gods, when we landed at the golden walls of the castle, *Heimdallr* saw me and the falcon, his golden teeth shone as he greeted me into his home, while the falcon shapeshifted into the goddess Freyja with her Falcon feathered cloak, the fire of *Muspelheims* locks that flew within her veiled waist shifted to face the sun of my bedraggled, baffled face. She then smiled and explained to me, "Mortal woman, Asa Embjørg, from this day on, you will be freed from Thralldom and be wedded to my brother, Freyr." As she ripped off my slave collar with her strong dagger, I earnestly questioned: "but what of his wife, Gerðr the giantess and her shimmering beauty?" " Freyrs love for Gerðr grew upon on bland physical attraction until both had grown tired of the relationship. Heimdallr then bid the guards to open the palace gates, and he bid us to seat ourselves, Freyja explained Freyr's impatience as she then lifted me on her golden chariot, the fact that I was 5"3 had dwarfed me in comparision to her 5"10, the golden chariot was pulled by her two cats, *Bygul* and *Trjegul,* as we rode through the effervescent city, she explains, "he bestows his heartsick love deeply upon you, he has seen pure light in your soul and bids to his presence in his hall". My heart suddenly began to beat out of it's chest, despite my still doubt, I have spend long nights dreaming of the sacred, holy king Freyr to bestow his peace and fair golden locks woven of the sun upon my cheek. I longed for his fair lips to smooth my rough, cracked ones. We then reached the edge and Freyja transformed into a falcon once again, clasped me and we glided away to Vanaheimr, the realm of Freyr's dwelling, as we flew, Freyja told me the story of the creation of the universe, starting from the wise one *Mmir*, we then landed on the mossy green foliage of Vanaheimr, we walked until Freyja reached her palace and left me to *Skirnir*, Freyr's servant who was transport me to Freyrs hall, we walked until I asked him about Gerors reaction after the divorce, he darkly laughed and said that Geror never wanted the marriage to occur, but the marriage happened after a series of threats from himself and from his magical wand, *Gambanteinn,* he began by telling me what he recalled saying to her, it was the following

"Seest thou, maiden, this keen, bright sword,

That I hold here in my hand?

Before its blade the old giant bends,—

Thy father is doomed to die.

I strike thee, maid, with my gambanteinn,

To tame thee to work my will;

There shalt thou go where never again

The sons of men shall see thee."

I suddenly shivered at the thought of leaving Freyr, even though I already had deeply loved him, If i wronged him, I would possibly be cursed to be unwed or to be married to a three headed giant.

We stopped at a large, mossy tree, I opened my sack and ate my biscuit bread and crabapples, vegetables and Skirnir offered me his stories, I was showing him my woven cloths when my curiousity then appealed me at the sight of the *Ängsälvor* , or meadow elves dancing in a circle-dance in clairvoyant white robes in the swaying, green meadows that stretched to the end of time, I walked the circle to get a closer look when someone touched my shoulder, and a strong, deep and rich voice proclaimed:

"I now behold forth a maiden dear to me, and the gleam of her soul shone all the sea and sky."

Turning around to see, my breath was caught in the warmth of Freyrs amber eyes,

"To me more dear than in days of old was ever maiden to man; but no one of gods or elves will grant That we be together should be."

And with that, his lips were gently pressed to mine. He wrapped me into his large, muscled and strong arms and held me closely to his bare, strong chest that draped over with clear white linen, my skin felt warm and my heart was racing intensely, I lifted my eyes to meet his and we latched them forever, I knew I would not have to say a word as i knew, in the depth of the chambers of my heart, that it was love as he laid me down into the swaying grass of desire.

I awakened the next morning with Freyr's wide arms still wrapped around me, he slowly opened his eyes and smiled at me, pulling my head towards his and tousling my hair, still wary and doubtful, whispered "out all of the fair maidens and goddesses, why have you bestowed your love and desire upon my filthiness?" his face was angered, and held me closer, "filthy?! from the second time I sat, with stealth, upon *Hlithskjalf,* Odins throne when he was away, I looked upon the strength in your courtesy and kindness despite being treated like chattel, Asa, your radiant, beautiful heart and soul was what made me fall in love with you, for the one night that I had spent after the first time I had seen you was long enough, yet longer still are two; how then shall I contend with three? for months have passed more quickly than half a bridal eve," tightening his hands around my neck, I saw the wild passion enflame in his eyes as he continued: "my obsession for you grew stronger as my mind turned wilder, I could not sleep in normalty as vivid dreams of you flooded my head, but mortals and gods could not love as it was considered taboo. but I defied tradition and divorced Gerd" his face then increased in vitality and pressed his lips deeply to mine and said "you will be my one and only one until the day of Ragnarok." He then helped me up and gave an intricately sewn, luminous white dress and a woven golden, knotted belt and delicate veil, "my love's glimmering beauty is not equivalent to this tunic's cow manure."

A year passed as I lived with Freyr in his palace, we lived with our child, Bjorn, a child with fair skin and shining dark hair locks symmetric to mine, and with the intense, amber eyes of the same warmth and strength of his father. The role of a mother's responsibility was indifferent to me, as I had done the most of raising Rögnveig, I had treasured the child through through every string of my heart, pouring out into my motherly love for my son and passionate love for my true, eternal beloved Freyr. As I rode out on my horse, covered in my white, linen veil, iridescent with the snow of my dress, I rode through the lush Vanaheimr, as I imagined in the distance, meadow elves would be dancing in the green meadows, hearts singing the melodies of the stars.

Light

I remember waiting at the subway station, before the train halted its journey
of motion, as the sparks of friction flew off the wheels, and the masses of
people flooded into the cabins and became one with the train, perhaps you
could say that the train symbolizes humans, and the motion of the train
symbolizes the flowing river, which possesses each human internal journey
and how they all stream to the same ocean of souls that drift from the
physical world. After arriving to my destination , I entered the taxi and was
driven to a beautiful, green land of hills, I had found an Inn and stayed in a
calm, quiet, but homely room, I slipped on my white, loose embroidered
cotton nightgown, after taking a nap that developed into soft sleep. I woke
up the next day to a beautiful morning, as I looked out the window and saw
white fireflies, slowly dancing, as if, drunk on golden sunshine. I remember
feeling the cool fresh air, it was the simplest beauty, far greater than the
greatest material wealth, to simply breathe the crisp air through my nostrils.
It was as if those fireflies danced to the music of their own souls, with not a
care in the world except flowing with the river that was the flowing language
of their souls, imagine, reader, that water was overflowing out of the cup it is
in, you would feel scared because the overflowing water might cause a mess,
but isn't that what we are afraid of? that the naked truth of our soul,
represented by the water, would spill? whether that naked truth would cause
chaos or it would shine a beautiful light, at some point, it must be embraced,
a whisper in our hearts of the truth of our selves, a truth that can drive us
from the surface of the facade that we show to other humans and into the
depths of the whole honesty of who you are. Like a bird being set free from
a cage, let your true colours shine through the night, the same night in which
I spoke to the rain, I told the rain, I am human, who are you? to which the
rain replied, well, you could say physically you are human, spiritually, you
are not, every drop of me is a multitude of atoms, as are you, when I fall and
return from the ocean to the sky, so will you, when I showered my clear
crystal drops on the leaves of grass, as soft dew of the stars, I will return to
the apple and fig orchards, the iridescent haze of dawn, that will soon turn
into sunrise of your soul's chant of the light and shadows, aurora and mist,

the coloured strata of clouds, that stream with the waves, as you look at the horizon, reader, I am not speaking to the rain, but to my soul, and your souls, that speak to the sea of creation, space and time.

Lotus

I am a little structure, my fins silken through the waters of my mind, flowing through the neurons of my brain, connected together like humans in the tapestry of life, i follow the pathways and swim with platelets, like fish shining their silvery scales in the river that flows as i evolve, from a little structure to an Amoeba, you would think, how could a structure with fins evolve into a finless one? well, the truth is, reader, the human will evolve when enlightened with the shower of wisdom that they already possess the treasure, that is the wings of their inner self, then, they will have no need to show themselves through any other way. The way through which I had swam, the Amoeba, in the tissue of stars, within the greater nucleus of the universe.

Close your eyes, reader, in the idyll of your inner peace, gentle sunlight breaks from the clouds, touching the ocean of your soul, that lingers on the water's surface, where the lotus blossom blooms in the indigo twilight.

See the clear layer of the ocean, take a look into its glass surface, reader, see how it reflects you, a structure, like me, in the greater sea of time, before we eventually disperse into matter, which is the ocean, through which we are spirits in harmony, like the flower and the sun that flows through homes, that shelters souls, and through every soul shelters its own home. The essence of dark, is light, the Aurora Borealis is a cavilcade of iridescence, you awe at its beauty, as love flows through and you open completely through your eyes, sometimes the colour of emotion is within the purity of the gaze, light illuminates from the mist of language, that speaks to the human spirit, in higher waves of transcendence of your inner self, the human, immune of speech, will only let love through the heart, the heart of the universe.

<u>Lovers</u>

She thought of how eyes see both the unity and parting of lovers, the flames that burn through hearts and the flames that scorch. Eyes see the ripples of the sea of war, in all of its forms, the sea of tears, the sea of love, in which we are all organisms under the sea of stars.

As she walked through the fields, she remembered his eyes, green eyes, clear and bright, like the the effervescent foam of the river flowing down through the aqua shower of light.

Suddenly, she felt the breath of the wind calling her spirit, she ran through the long, swaying grass, hearing the heart of her lover whispering her name, she began running as she had longed to escape her emotional poverty and return to the embracing arms of her lover, and let him passionately kiss her soul.

She ran until she heard the whispers ceasing and she saw the mist unfold from the hill, unveiling a figure that stood there, the red rose blooms from the thorns of her heart as she saw the sun softly glowing the light, fair skin of Alastair, her lover.

"Eve" he called as he ran towards her and embraced her. She touched his soft, light fair hair, they held each others hands as they walked back to his home.

"I have not seen you in years, Alastair, I have desperately missed you...but I knew I had to move on after you found a new woman, was her name Emily?"

"Me and Emily had a troublesome relationship, so the relationship was ended, but i do not wish to talk about Emily now, to be honest, every fruitless moment i was with her, I have missed you very much..."

At this point in the conversation, Alastair and Eve reached the house and they sat down on his couch,

"Would you like some tea, Eve?"

"Yes, i would", she replied as he came back a few minutes with two mugs of tea, "you remembered that vanilla tea is my favorite, Alastair" Eve said.

Alastair smiles and then replies "I did, next to your second preferred drink, milk and honey" in his rich, deep voice, she felt the warmth of his breath as his soft, full lips kiss her cheek, and his green eyes glow luminescent of love.

"I love you, Alastair" she whispered, as dawn fades into the sea of night, Alastair wraps his arms around Eve, he held her close, as she slowly began to sleep, he softly whispered back, "And I love you too, Eve."

Fire

Reader, we set the scene with the clear, chilling gust thrusting against Helena's pale skin as she lifted the gown to crush through the thick blanket of snow under crystal-veined leaves. In the forest of a Manor owned by a man of the name Mr.Smith, she walked down a lone path lined by fresh, almost frozen overgrown moss, suddenly, a horse had shrieked like blazing of a bonfire, she ran towards the sound and saw a man, the rider, struggling to get up from a broken tree bark, she rushed towards him and tried to help him up, "I will get help, sir.." but before she could, he forcefully pushed her hand away "thank you, but I can support myself" "no sir, your injuries are a clear like a river wide, you need to healed, and I will not stop until you recieve treatment". After a deep sigh from the stranger, he said "you have a steadfast stubborn nature that is admirable, but I don't see how I would need help from your small frame, perhaps we can go down to the local hospital" "located where?" she asked, "In the village of Perthshire", she silently sighed to myself, "If his cooperation was as great as his ego, he would win a United Kingdom championship."

She left the man at the hospital and arrived at the Smith manor, she lifted her gown and petticoat and rode through the eternal, deep stories woven in the lush green hills, Helena had a modest house in Edinburgh which formed no contrast to the eerie, rich simplicity of th Smith manor. She arrived at the prominent, oak wood front doors, Helena knocked and Mr.Knobbs, a servant, opened the doors, she entered to a home that was lined with carpets of deep rich,scarlet rugs of velvet fabrics, a few dark paintings, the hallways were tall, wide, yet it was as if the light, clear white embroidered curtains spoke a deep, untold fate about this house.

"Ms.Carter!" Jane Smith, the sister of John, had rushed to embrace Helena with her bouncing blonde curls, "are you well? you are extremely late for dinnertime, are you cold?" Helena had explained to her what happened, but she paid no attention to it and took her to the dining room.

As the Knife sliced through the moist, thick meat, Jane's blonde lashes flicked up, the storm of her eyes calmed against the dark earth of Helena's.

"My brother requests to meet you after dinner, you may prepare yourself"

Helena then returned to her bedroom, she tightened her corset, chemise and flaming red petticoat and evening gown with a very low neckline, though, the minute she had lifted the mirror, the color had drained from her face, unlike the ravishing female nymphs and characters she drew in her notebooks, as she removed her enormous, feather- and flower-laden poke bonnet

and she saw a long face with a plain nose,dark eyes and hair, her hair was not as thick and curly as the Noblewomen, she thought to myself of how she was a fool to impress Mr.Smith, and got out of the door with her dress trailing behind her like blood. Reader, Mr.Smith was a 39 year old Nobleman who inherited the land from his deceased father, Reverend Smith, the whole of U.K celebrated him at their parties and gatherings and spoke of his fathers good, grand charity achievements, yet under the bursting of color and laughter of 18 to 20 year old noblemen and noblewomen, Mr.Smith scorned it all. As he rode in a carriage back to the Smith manor, he was reaching the entrance, he greeted Mr.Knobbs, his servant of 10 years, "good day, sir, I trust you had a safe trip from Edinburgh?" as Mr.Knobbs tipped his Bowler hat, Mr.Smith

greeted him back with a cold, indifferent smile and the same smile was given for his sister, whom smiled but he knew, from the depths within him, that she cared for nothing but material wealth.

He sat down on his bed with a deep, heavy sigh, he removed his outer clothing, hanging his black top hat. Reader, as he placed his hand on his heart and he felt through his chemise, beneath the strings of his heart, where there was a ember that was dying out, a ember that longed to be unleashed from still, numb, bottomless space. He was informed that they had a guest tonight, Ms. Helena Carter, the daughter of his deceased Father's loyal friend, he dressed himself in his finest, crisp black double breasted vest and turnover collar shirt with a four in hand necktie, dark trousers and breeches. Even though, compared to wealth of his clothing, his heart was in entrenched poverty.

Helena was led by Jane to a room lit by a fireplace aflame, she saw a wide, but athletic and strong frame sitting in a velvet, tall chair, Jane introduced her and a deep, surrounding voice asked her quietly to leave and for Helena to sit. She passed the chair of Mr.Smith. Reader, with a flick of her eye, she saw his craggy, tired countenance under a thick, fiery reddish-golden, flaxen brow, his light brown eyes seem to show beneath the depths that he was deeply depressed. She then sat down and their eyes met.

Mr.Smith instantly recognized Helena's dark, calm demeanour, yet presently, she had a determined fire of chivalry in her eyes, with the glowing white fire of her fair skin revealed by her low neckline, like the celestial elves of Asgard in Norse Myth.

She was smiling now at him and he realized that he had forgotten to speak, he did what he had not done for so many years, and blushed intensely as he tried to begin the conversation by asking her common knowledge questions of where she came from, her past, and occupation.

She explained that her name is Helena Carter, she was born in York and, with the acceptance of her family, had moved to Scotland after gaining a decent amount of money from her recent novel, Fire, and explained that she was a writer of novels. Instead of telling him the story, she smiled elfishly and said that never in his wildest fancies would she ever give the story away for the first time, they then continued to talk for hours, Mr.Smith then began to turn very arrogant and prideful, which can be a sin at times,

"But I have achieved more experiences than you will ever have, as you suck on the mothers breast like a newborn". She raised her dark eyebrows in surprise, "but do you understand and have immersed yourself truly in these experiences, Mr.Smith?" "I have lived them! have you not heard me, Ms. Carter?" he replied in surprising vigour, slight defiance enflaming in his deepened brow. "understanding is a very powerful sense that many misuse, Mr.Smith, and once you connect experiences with yourself, you can shape yourself" "I have been experiencing understanding and acceptance for many years, life has turned on me."

"How?" "Well, Ms.Carter, after my fathers death, people then set their values upon me, they set upon the high values of what my father represented, charitable, good, calm.."

He darkly smiled, "I was nothing alike to his persona"

Helena, mockingly, and in a bursleque fashion, acted surprised and said "No! you truly have shocked me, Mr.Smith!"

He breathed in and continued, "yes, my dear Ms.Carter, that was exactly how i was, brash, young and untamed, and from a city, even, if you came from a farm, you would be more quiet."

She intensifed her stare "But, I am nothing like a spoiled, brash noble, Mr.Smith, I have not set myself higher than others so that I would stoop to a lower level, trust me, I am not your general type, Mr.Smith". He smiled, genuinely for the first time after many seasons and years and replied, "You speak truth, none from human species have I found in you" as he thought to himself, "what wild, untamed feeling has seizes me the moment I beheld an elf like her?" he then said to her "I wish for you to call me by my first name, Aidan" "Your name is Aidan? that does not seem like a typically british name" "My scottish grandfather's name was Aidan, so my father named me after him, in his honor" Helena with a calm and quiet eye, seemed to notice a stranger flicker in his eyes under thick wavy lock of flames, his back was not pressed to the chair but now leaning slightly towards her, taking long minutes of time to look at her, as the flames in his eyes blended with dark earth, such as two worlds blending like water" they immersed themselves into the depth of conversations, eyes flickering like stars, swimming in the seas of each other like fish in clear aqua, waves crashing before Helena was softened back to reality and reminded herself of the time and knew that she was to retire to bed, she explained to him, he set his firm, squared jaw and said "you are dismissed".

As the days passed by, Helena found that Mr. Smith requested her presence more and more, as Helena and Aidan's relationship grew, Jane's sky blue eyes looked upon the couple from a balcony afar, they seemed so fair, but struck like daggers, sharpening her gaze more and more every week that Jane and Aidan spent time together. Until one night, Reader, Helena had slept in her bed, until she awoke and felt cold silver, heartbeats adrenalized from her heart to the skin that was touched by the dagger of Jane Smith, "My brother was sound as a rock, until you came and ruined everything!" the silver was about to slither before Jane was grabbed by Aidan and taken out of her room. She heard his pounding feet up to the basement and the locking of the basement door behind him, and rushing down the stairs to Helena's room, he rushed down and held her wrists in reassurance "I trust you are well?" and then grabbed a glass casket and poured water and she took it as her free, small hand was held by his thick, muscled one, and she barely whispered as she was still in the aftermath of shock and exhaustion "Is there.." "shhh.." as he gently placed his palm on Helenas cheek and placed her skin against his "Being there for you, that's all I will need and I shall never ask anything in return, I knew something was missing inside of me, Helena, and the first time I beheld you the first night, I saw an angel". She was about to leave his hand as she knew it was getting late before he said, "You are leaving?" "yes, my hands are cold," when in fact, Helena felt like her body was melting into warm gradients of a summer sunset, she retired to her bed, opening her eyes slightly, she found that Aidan was gone.

Helena dreamed that she dancing upon dandelions, delicate and swirling through the milky twilight like an unfurling carnation, until she was awoken by the bell, she arised her petite frame from the thick blankets and done her dark mane into a braid and joined Mr.Smith for a breakfast of freshly ground biscuits, English tea and fresh apricot jam from the Manor's gardens. Helena greeted him and he greeted Helena back with a smile and said: "Good Morning, sweet sounding skylark. I would sometimes ask myself if you were real? but I was wild in desire and hallucination to behold such a fiery, celestial spirit encased in such yet seemingly calm demeanour? nestle, divine spirit, to my withered heart!" Helena could not help but smile "You have too much spirit to be withered, my dear, let us revive those leaves and let them float back to the tree, the tree of life!"

Helen and Edward then walked through the wheat fields, where he then proposed to her, she accepted blissfully and their lips passionately enterwined to one another, dew flowed down their skin as they quenched their endless thirst.

Until Helena had found the paper, she was returning with Edward to the Manor and she found a paper of a letter Edward had written to his lover in his room, she felt as if every vein had squeezed and burned with the fire of scandal, she knew was set to have a tragic ending after her lover parted her in the cold wind of the facade of a juvenile mind, she threw the paper and ran away from the Manor to the stables, "Helena! Helena!" Aidan screamed as he ran to search for her with burning, scorching tears in his flaming heart, Helena had returned to Edinburgh and now had a reason to complete her book.

Reader, she did not have a change of heart until until many years later, when Helena finally decided to forgive him, she bought a trip back to England, she rode back to the Smith Manor, and found the Manor burned into ashes like a dying phoenix, she learned from the servants that were saved by Mr.Smith that the house was burned by Jane who crashed the door open and burned

the manor, Edward escaped, but only through crashing through the bottom window of the palace, leaving him with an injured chest that required extensive surgery, he survived after being blessed by a miracle, Helena was told that he now he lives by himself in Perthshire. She took the directions to the destination and rode down the same path that she took when she first healed Mr.Smith from his wounds by taking him to the hospital.

She knocked on the cottage door and the door opened to an older, weary looking woman, known later by Helena as the owner of the small home and a former servant of Mr.Smith's manor, they sat down and spoke about the huge enquality between the rich and poor. And if not for the money that was left with Mr.Smith before the rest was burned by Jane...she wouldn't

have even got a small cottage. Helena entered a fireplace lit room, where the same wide frame was sitting by a fireplace with a bandaged chest, she leaned her head to see him, and saw his countenance of the sunken seas of his entrenchment in anguish and depression, hidden by scorn in his brow, Helena placed the tray on the table in front of the fireplace and suddenly Aidan jumped from his seat, though deeply shrieking in pain before she tried to support him, he held her neck so intensely she felt choked, "WHERE HAVE YOU BEEN?!" with tears falling down his face, "I SEARCHED FOR YOU FOR SEASONS AND YEARS! DO NOT EVER LEAVE ME AGAIN!" he half cried, half shrieked in pain as she held his face and told him "you are my heart, my deepest passion and deepest love, when I left, I felt the deep strike of woe and anguish, even though I never forgave you, you stayed in my heart forever, I will never, never leave you again" tears fell down her face and into her heart as Aidan held her soft, dark velvet hair to him and kissed her more ardent in passion than ever before. The next morning, Helena woke up to a full, wavy fire tossed locks on the crisp white sheets, he slowed opened his light brown eyes full of warmth, Reader, the most blissful months they had spent together, Helena had borne a child, George, and the family, despite the fact that they didn't have much money, had the one pure gold they shared together.

Mandarin De Neilly: A Night Of Zen

It was a cold, wintery Paris night, after growing tired of my uncle's constant repitition of the question on what i wanted to eat, i finally decided upon chinese food, he did not tell me the name of the restaurant, he just told me "I know this great place to eat chinese food, lets go!" as me and my family walked the almost endless, wide sidewalks of Paris and we reached a small restaurant, 2 golden, neon signs glowed the sign "Mandarin De Neilly", a small square building with large windows was headed by the small front sign that was placed above the restaurant entrance, and the back sign was larger and was seated on the old, abandoned french building in which the restaurant was built. The restaurant looked authenticly chinese, adorned with neon glow chinese letters paired next the front sign, red chinese designs garnish the bottom of the restaurant, under the large, clear windows in which you could clear see the gentle, golden framing on the glass that encased golden paint on the wall of the restaurant. As the french people quietly eating their meals in wooden chairs, eating their food on the tablecloth covered wooden tables, above them, chinese lanterns that contained a thousand fireflies merging to become the sun that illuminated our presence as we walked in. We entered the small restaurant that opened to us an ancient chinese temple, marble vases garnished by an elaborate floral design, wreathed around the area of the vase where bright red pots held the soil of green vining aloe vera leaves that sprouted flowers that were iridescent white under the lanterns encased with wooden, chinese design, in the foreground sat unconnected a small, bronze and gold wall embroidered with detailed chinese designs, in front of the wall was another golden, chinese lantern that lit the silky orange scales of the fish flowing through the light that touches the embroidered traditional chinese calligraphy painted on the red sign. The atmosphere of zen flowed through the first slice of my fork on the rich golden, sweet pineapple sauce glazed on the moist, juicy duck, it was cut in thin slices even though its juices melted through my tongue that savoured the sugar of pineapple moist with the taste of the duck. I had paired it with a summer roll, crunchy and golden with the taste of delicious, scrumptious duck pieces and hot steamed white rice. The dinner ended with a calm, light green tea, i insisted upon putting sugar, because i love putting sugar in my tea or coffee, unlike others who prefer their coffee sour for some strange reason i just never understood, who wants their coffee without sugar? anyway, the green tea was delicate and smooth silk on my tongue, a light shade of green delicated wreathed with the flower of jasmine, if you nudged your nose a bit close, you can smell the fresh life of the jasmines wreathed with the leaf green of the tea. I closed my eyes, sunlight seams through my skin, its arms caress me in warmth, the tea purifying me as i close my eyes and heavenly pleasure enfolds my soul in a bed of pleasure, my consciousness dissolves to a higher state of mind, the delicacy of the jasmine through the golden liquid melted through my tongue, blossoming my taste buds, it's tranquility made me feel like i ran barefoot with the wind, that explodes a thousand florets into the sky, like a thousand musical notes into the sea of the sky that housed the earth, the same earth of the tea that made me imagine myself walking down the forest path, the "Iris" of my eye glimmers euphoria, much like the Greek goddess herself, sun silk seams through my skin, and through the flowing river that shimmers fishscales like a sheet of diamond, my fingers, nimble as a lark, run through tree bark, surround sound waves, radiate natures unseen energy, my naked feet squish the soil, that vines out the blessings of God upon the earth, the earth peripherating in this tea. In my consciousness, the tea droplets flew into the sky, as her toes splashed the pond in the distance, i smiled and felt my skin glow warm as she watched the flamingos fly into the sunset, rising, beautiful, delicate ascension towards the light, their wings floating as i watch from the glimmer of the lone sea stone, a glowing haze, golden, crimson skies, i was lifted from the sea and with the birds i flew. I opened my eyes, the sunset rose within my eyes as the warm glow of the chinese lanterns illuminating the atmosphere of "Mandarin Neilly" that flowed through memories i will never forget, as my uncle ordered the bill, we began to retreat from the haven of zen towards the calm, night ocean of Paris.

Nymphea

Her dark hair flowed out of the freshwater reflecting a layer of sun. Her white dress floating in the depth of the clear fields of sound waves surrounding the invisible sea of sky. Warmth enveloped through her consciousness, evaporating into the mist that glowed one leaf transparent and then another through the birds' songs running together with the interlacing of the mountain stream whose waters foam on the beach shore. She closed her eyes, and let her consciousness immerse into the dew of the green grass, gently swaying to the wind merging with sky, painted with the mist of language through the veins of leaves spread through the glowing anatomy of the mystical Garden Of Eden.

The bare, sun lit feet of James had walked through the the old grecian columns wreathed with the roses that spread through the lush, green foliage of eternity. The sounds of the rainforest in the garden surrounded his ears. He closed his eyes as dew trickles upon the leaves, he was immersed in the rainbow ribbons rippling through the reflecting light of hibiscus dew. He was lost in the energy of the rising spirits of euphoria as he exhaled and he opened my eyes, the zen had gently massaged his consciousness, that was drifting in the sea of rose petals. He contempelated that the ripples on the water are circular like the moon, glowing through the wings of his soul opening, the golden aura of the Garden Of Eden flowed through his long, fair hair.

He had a knit, brown burlap sack, taking from the rich abundance of apples, marigolds, berries, milk from the cows in the fields far from the old grecian columns, in addition to a soft suede book bound by a string where he would write poetry and draw, "It is a shame that the beauty of Earth is slowly being destroyed" he thought to himself,
his bare, sun light feet walked through the moss lined path until he reached a lake, the green ground glimmered of dew forming a sheet of emerald. He lay his sack down on the floor and slept by the shore of the lake as the sun disappeared through the mist.

She saw a fair, golden strand dancing through the clear water, she tousled it until James felt the gentle pull and awoke, his flaxen lashes met her dark brown eyes and fair, porcelain skin,

"What is your name?", he asked

"Celeste", she replied

"What is your species"

" I am part of the Naiads" she then proceeded to trace on the ground "you can also write it like this in ancient greek and wrote down Ναϊάδες

"I am a type of the water nymphs (female spirits) called Naiads who preside over fountains, wells, springs, streams, brooks and other bodies of fresh water. I am a Leimenid, and I preside over lakes, what is your name?"

"My name is James"

"Tell me why you came to the Garden Of Eden"

"Because i wanted to escape from the abyss of my self-destruction"

Celeste's eyes increase in concern, "The human anatomy and soul is perfect in its own beauty, why would it want to destruct itself?"

"Because of the ravenous environment, in which the world will pressure you into the crushing depths of transformation"

"But you have a choice to transform yourself for the better, leave society to fend for its own, James, your human soul is beautiful, and society does not possess the upper hand, you possess the upper hand over the molding of your own being, for the same way that you can destruct yourself, you can let yourself break"

"Break?"

"Yes, James, to break, like the breaking up of rainbows into particles of blossom"

She continued, "Have you ever marveled, James, that when the eyes first open from sleep, it is like the opening of a dozen monarchs and swallowtails that fly into the sky?"

"How is like, to think as a Leimenid would?"

"Thoughts through my mind flow like Koi fish in clear water"

She then said, "In fact, your eyes are beautifully clear"

He smiled, "Thank you, and yours are powerful and allude to quiet wisdom, like the earth, as your hair is the waters of the night ocean above"

His smile slowly faded,

"Why does your smile fade, James?"

"Because, despite my percieved outer beauty, no one truly had loved me, except for my family of course, because of the person i am on the inside, Celeste"

"James, i understand that you have something in your world called Yin and Yang, am I correct?"

"Yes, it's true"

"Yin is darkness, and Yang is light, the butterfly blooms from the cocoon when it has seen the light in the darkness"
His smile slightly returned, "Thank you for your advice"
"The Night is long, do you not you think you need sleep?"
"You are right, I do"
And so he returned to his slumber, and Celeste dissolved into the lake.

Tears of the dew flowed down from the leaves and into Celeste's heartstrings that transformed into the green enterwining vines rooting from depths of the lake, sprouting a scarlet bud at the surface.

James awoke and saw that Celeste was gone and wept for days, for he had loved Celeste and never had the chance to tell her, his tears flowed through the lake, that wreathed his tears into the leaves of the scarlet rose that unfolded and detached from the vine, floating towards James, who cradled the rose and held it to the sky, it floated and from its petals bloomed the auric portal to Earth, the blue-green marbled sphere periperating in the eyes of James, he took one step forward into the portal, and James was launched through the multi-coloured path until he landed in the sea, he was realized that he was in Australia and not far from shore and swam until his fingers touched the golden grains of the sand that whispered to him,
"Your heart has wept over Celeste, but little did you know that she dissolved into the waters because she wept for you as well"
"Why did she weep for me?" he asked
"Because when she said that your eyes are beautifully clear, she had not spoken of your eyes in a physical sense, James, she had fallen deep in love because in the depth of your eyes, she saw the clarity of her own beauty reflected".

Poetry Of The Soul

Chapter 1

Jane immersed herself in the waters of the bath, immersed in the silence of sound that surrounded her being and rendered her floating in the bridge between unconsciousness and consciousness.

The scarlet rose blooms in the swirling dark tempest, as she slowly emerged to the surface, she patted herself dry and slipped on her nightgown and drank her French Vanilla tea. Jane was not a lonely person, but her friends tried to push her towards online dating, but for some reason, many of the young men her friends suggested seemed to be less cultured or mature-minded than herself, or seemed to be too typical or unoriginal. Upon sipping her tea, she arose as her bare, small feet shrouded the float of her pure white nightgown. Walking towards the skyscraper glass to contemplate the milky way twilight of the New York city sky.

Suddenly, her laptop sounded a notification. It was from the online dating website, it had suggested a man named Nicholas.

Jane had believed in her will deciding her destiny, for Rilke had written in "Letters To A Young Poet" that "Destiny itself is like a wonderful wide tapestry in which every thread is guided by an unspeakably tender hand, placed beside another thread, and held and carried by a hundred others." She began typing, and so the conversation begins.

Chapter 2

 -Dear Nicholas,
Understand my secret love for poetry, late night tea, fascination in the tiny details. My love shining through flames that warmly embraces the soul glowing through my chest that is raised to meet the sun that spreads through spirits of euphoria, transcending me through the aura of Zen. That immerses us together in the sea of life.-
 -With Love, Jane

 -Dear Jane,
You speak of Life, which is like the flash of a firefly in the night, it glows through the dew of wildflower. It is the breath of a winter wolf, it is the

unseen shadow which runs across the grass and loses itself in the sunset. But i would like to know, what is your opinion on Love?-
    -With Love, Nicholas

    -Dear Nicholas,
Love is the warmth of the fabric of cashmere that slips on the skin, it dissolves through you and embraces in its arms, its embers glow through the skin, arms are raised to the sky, and become one with the sun. I have not inquired your opinion yet, Nicholas, what do you think of Thought, could it perhaps be interrelated to the eyes?-
    -With Love, Jane

    -Dear Jane,
You ask an intelligent question, and i shall answer by saying that eyes are the glass windows that mirror emotions, and true self. I shall give you an example, Jane, for like the pond and it's surface, the surface of the pond mirrors your actions and behavior.Thus, beneath the surface of the pond, your true self and emotions simmer in the depth.Jane, you are an intelligent young woman,but do you possess depth in imagination?-
    -With Love, Nicholas

    -Dear Nicholas,
I so dearly close my eyes, and dissolve myself in the cool, fresh waters of my imagination. I close my eyes, and the sun glints against the water droplets that fly through the sky as my toes splash the pond in the distance. I smile to myself as i, in my imagination, raise my arms and feel the sun glow my skin warm as i watch the swans fly into the sunset.Nicholas, tell me of about the human eye-
    -With Love, Jane

Chapter 3

    -Dear Jane,
What do you see when you look Into the human eye? You see plainly an eye.....I see the windows to the soul that ignites of the cosmos, I see the periphery of the Wildflower dew that glimmers against sun streams, i see how the elements of the creations of God that are found in both Animals and Humans and beings of the universe. I see the graceful force of the Eagle extending it's wings towards the Sun, Jane in your eyes I see colors of emotion they shine rainbow strobe lights that resonate with mine, take my

hand, Jane together we will burst into the universe. Will you tell me about your eyes, Jane?
   -With Love, Nicholas

   -Dear Nicholas,
Take one look at my dark brown eyes, what do you see? a shrouded wall of strength streaked with independence's fire, a shrouded wall of strength, the wall guards oceans of my emotions.Sensitivity to the sunshine on hibiscus dew drops, as you see me walking down the pavement, shrouded beneath a baggy sweater, what do you see?
You see what you want to believe.
   With Love, Jane

   -Dear Jane,
Your words do strike me, but tell me of your Nirvana.-
   -With Love, Nicholas

   -Dear Nicholas,
If that is what you wish, I shall tell you of how i lay in the scarlet sheets of Roses, as i bask in soft skin caress, I shall tell you of the immersion into dance between petals, as the roses bloom their inner scents, as i open my eyes to Nirvana. Tell me of what brings you pleasure, Nicholas.-
   -With Love, Jane

   -Dear Jane,
I am pleasured by showers, as i turn the knob, trickling dews of sunlight flow down my body, bonfire arms encompass my being in their warmth, i smile to myself and i realized i've spent too long in the shower, i pat myself dry, however, Jane, the warm feeling still glows through me, wherever i go.-
   -With Love, Nicholas

Chapter 4

   -Dear Nicholas,
You speak soft words, soft as the glide of the gentle wings of the swallows that explode through the sky like a thousand musical notes, Nicholas, tell me about Music, what is special about Music to you?-

-With Love, Jane

-Dear Jane,
Being a musician myself, Music is an aurora of colours, the essence of song comes from the human subconscious, it is an instincual feeling and music to the soul can be what a water bath does to the body, like a water bath, music can cleanse the soul of sadness.Jane, tell me, what brings you sadness?-
　　-With Love, Nicholas

-Dear Nicholas,
 Sadness for me is seeing how corrupt governmental officials bring upon their savage rule upon innocent citizens, and these presidents or officials do not see that being a true leader is different than being a president or official. Sadness for me is seeing racism, abuse, and more problems along with poverty in Third World countries, Sadness for me is seeing how Humans turn upon each other and sometimes, do not realize that forgiveness is not for just ending the conflict, but rather for achieving inner peace for the people in conflict. Now, tell me about what you think is peace, Nicholas?
　　-With Love, Jane

-Dear Jane,
Peace is when humanity sees that the power of love is greater than the love for power and wealth. Jane, your words speak truth, the truth that connects us through typed letters that flow through the electricity of our minds, Jane, tell me more about electricity, and the night.
　　-With Love, Nicholas

-Dear Nicholas,
I shall tell you that Electricity is when my body silhouettes against the pale moonlight, and i feel the energy of Nature's wildflower dew flowing through me, Electricity is when i raise my arms to the Night and feel my body sung electric. Electricity is when our fingers will touch, running through our heartbeats that ignites electricity through our veins, that glow neon lights flaming through the night, Nicholas tell me, what if the Galaxy was connected to Earth?
　　-With Love, Jane

Chapter 5

　　-Dear Jane,

Then Stardust would glimmer through the flashing headlights that glide through the New York tunnels, or warp-holes. Car horns would blast the birth of a star, the sound would explode solar flares through alleyways connecting like constellations, glimmering through headlights that form the iridisence of the Cosmos.

-With Love, Nicholas

-Dear Nicholas,
You can also say that the very tendrils of the Cosmos is within Humanity. Such as the tendrils of you that enbranch through my mind and enflame my memory. Oh, I wish that we could sit together, Nicholas, in the softness of a Hammock, Sun shining in our hair as we bath in our little infinity. Oh Nicolas, sometimes, I wish we could run wild together, what is wild to you, Nicholas?

-With Love, Jane

-Dear Jane,
Do you not know that wild is the flash of a firefly, its wings, crystalline and mystic, glowing through wildflower dew? and through the eyes of the wolf that whispers winter breath into the night that shields its own secrets? out of the darkness, wild horses, on the other side of the galaxy, Jane, will be unleashed, like the crashing flames of the burning roses of my passion for you, Jane, that has sung my body electric through the rage of my pulsating heart, Jane, that is wild.

With Love, Nicholas

-Dear Nicholas,
Wild is the fact that music is present in all things, and as Lord Byron had wrote, "There's music in all things, if men had ears, their earth is but an echo the spheres". And your words echoes through me, Nicholas, like the invisible surround sound of love that flows through Humanity. I also like "Echoes" by Pink Floyd, do you like Pink Floyd, Nicholas?

-With Love, Jane

-Dear Jane,
I love Pink Floyd, and i especially like the song "Comfortably Numb", I don't know if we can find a hammock, but maybe we can meet up in the "Carnation Cafe" here in Manhattan, New York city at 8:30. I'm light skinned, i have blond, longish hair, I'm 6 feet, I'm always wearing a long, cotton shirt and i have light blue eyes, slightly baggy jeans, full lips, and I'll

always have a CD player. I think it's sad that they don't make them anymore. Sometimes I feel like i'm alone because i think like that, how will identify you?
-With Love, Nicholas

-Dear Nicholas,
I am 5'3, straight dark brown hair, light skin, almond shaped dark brown eyes, I'll be wearing red lipstick placed upon a lower lip thats thicker than the upper, and i'll be a wearing a baggy, white wool sweater with light colored bootcut jeans. And dont worry, I'll find you Nicholas, you are not alone.
-With Love, Jane

Chapter 6

She had lain her pale arm on the glistening marble of of the baroque fountain nestling the prominent statue of Narcissus that centered the garden of the "Carnation Cafe". As Jane contemplated his countenance, she recalled the tale of Narcissus in "The Alchemist" by Khaled Husseini, wreathed with the call of the water nymph, whom claimed that "I wept for Narcissus as in the depth of his eyes, i saw my own beauty reflected".
-"Shall i compare thee to a winter's night.."
Jane's eyes arose to met the eyes of Nicholas,
"Thou art, Jane, more mysterious and pleasant,
In silent, still nights, so calm and lovely,
And overlooked as desolate,
Elegant winds, to and forth, sound through
Stars across the sky brought tessellate,
The luminous moon doth shine its beams pure
Falls the sound of fading soon to be past
Jane, Thy glorious magnificence rages
As i have sought for you throughout my ages"-
Jane smiled and said, "How could you have sought for me, Nicholas, when the souls conspire the meeting rather than the humans?". Their eyes met, as Nicholas's soul nestled against hers, She placed her small hand on his crisp white blouse, he held her close, and inhaled the vanilla scent of her soft-knit sweater, and began to tousle, the dark curls at the nape of her neck, he now performed unspoken words of affection, she felt the enfolding of the blanket of his love, the clear water glistened through the sky as they lay in the long,

green grass, wrapping themselves in their own cocoon, warmth of the flames inside unfolding through the cold night.

Chapter 7

"Jane?" Nicholas had whispered, "yes, Nicholas?" "Do you like Rumi's "The Book of Love?" " She smiled and was about to speak before he said, "I will not tell you now, but i will say that we must move out of the cafe because it is about to close down" And so Jane and Nicholas exited the cafe, Jane had told Nicolas that they will go to her house, however, a long time had passed and after Jane was almost going to stop walking, Nicholas told her "Keep walking, though there's no place to get to, don't try to see through the distances, that's not for human beings. Move within, but don't move the way fear makes you move" "You know, Nicholas, the minute i heard my first love story, I started looking for you, not knowing how blind that was. Lovers don't finally meet somewhere, They're in each other all along." "Nicholas, don't you realize that we are both quoting from Rumi's "The Book of Love"? but yes, it is true, Much like how the cosmos and the oceans are each other, Lovers are in each other as well. "Correct, now, do not speak" "Nicholas, Why?" "For you have unconsciously said what you are, I am what I am, your actions in my head, your head here in my hands, with something circling inside, i have no name for what circles so perfectly" Nicolas continued, "How the "sapling lifts, and the universe winds like a locust swarm its wingrush towards perfection "You have been quoting from Rumi's "The Book of Love" once again, but yet, Nicholas, it is perfect how the neurons of our minds are connected like the glimmering star constellations. Much like how inside water, a ripple vibrates through the auric glow of the moon" and we are swimming in the ocean of the night, and our souls are glowing a thousand candle flames". At this point, Jane and Nicolas had reached Jane's house, "But Nicholas, you won't attempt to..." "No, Jane, a real man would never attempt such a thing in the beginning stages of the relationship, we will soon get to know each other and then marry, unless, you have mistrust of me" "You fill my body and soul, Nicholas, i want nothing of this existence but our existence".

Chapter 8
After ordering pizza, Jane and Nicholas had spoken all night, as they had done in their online chat and their walk, Jane had then grown very tired and decided to sleep on the couch, Nicholas wrapped the blanket over her small frame, he then recited a part from a poem in Rumi's "Book of Love",

"Beyond day and night
One watches
As your eyes close and open and close,
As night turning day turns night, as eyes
Like particles float
In the light that is your face,
That is the sun"

Morning rose, and Jane, like a small animal, had lain curled up with her
closed eyes away from the sunlight streaming through the gentle blow of the
crisp white curtain, her long, dark eyelashes against the rose early morning
color of her skin. When she awoke, her small feet had reached the dining
table where, to her surprise, her breakfast had been made by Nicholas.
Her eyes lushly embraced the brioche, strawberry preserve, milk and eggs.
She ate with the flow of the butter to moisten the eggs and the coffee in the
fresh early morning texture.
After finishing, she had felt the warm arms of Nicholas whom has whispered
to her ear "I love you", Jane then replied, "I love you too, and I hear nothing
in my ear but your voice, your heart has broken my mind into a thousand
pieces" "and those thousand pieces would be..." "The flames of the sun that
rises" Jane then continued " above the collective existence of souls in the
universe like the connectivity of cells in the human tissues" He smiled and
said, "You are my equal and likeness, Jane, Let us marry and get away from
here"
"A dream yet to come alive, Nicholas, but first we need to get to know each
other more, in addition the approval of our families before getting married".
Pause. And fast forward to many months later.

Chapter 9
Jane looked out towards the sea of Cannes, she then looked at Nicholas
sleeping on the sand, fingers through the grains of sand that were beginning
to blow delicately with the rising wind when her feet stirred. She then laid
next to him, her delicate hands feeling his long, light cotton shirt. Soon, their
souls and the waves crashing upon their skin became one.
Nicholas's long, flaxen lashes arose to meet the sun, the ocean of his eyes
flowing of the interwoven transparent calligraphy of love. He then found
Jane seated, reading a book called "Jane Eyre" by Charlotte Bronte in the
balcony chair of their honeymoon beach house. "Dear, you should read this
book, it's very interesting" "How convenient that the character is named after
you?" She smiled, "Except for the last name" "What's the use of having a

last when our souls live forever?" Nicholas pondered. "Nicholas, let us go inside"

And so they went into the beach house, Nicholas laid the white sheet over Jane as they lay together, his arm under her head, he felt her cheek stroke against his, it felt silky as the gentle sound of the ocean waves through their ears and through the serenity of their beings.

Nicholas then awoke Jane and bought the *Chasseur Francais* and the *Miroir des Sports* and Jane had bought the new French *Vogue* and they drank cafe au lait.

As they spoke, a stunning woman with brilliantine hair walked past their table,

"How come you could not notice such a radiant woman, Nicholas?"

"Because she can have the most beautiful face and body,
but without the sphere of inner beauty, and in that case,
her's would not shine as much as yours, outer beauty
would be a mere facade like the marble statue of
Narcissus."

"Because he was so drowned in his outer beauty that he fell into the water"

"Do you remember the first time we met, Nicholas?"

"Yes, i do Jane, we would lay in the grass, and bathe in our own little infinity".

Chapter 10

They returned to the beach house, where they lay on the beach on the golden sand, Nicholas put some almond oil on the palm of his hand and spread it lightly with his fingers over the girls thighs and they glowed warm as the skin took the oil.

They then returned to the sun-lit balcony of the beach house, The large window was open and the warm, salty wind blew the crisp white curtain as Nicholas closed the door of the ice chest and poured 2 glasses of cool water, were they sat on the wooden seats, watching the sunset fade into the sea.

River
Ending Scene

From her outdoor balcony, River looked towards the sunset, she raised her lamp, its periphery glowing through the air flickering and flaming orange, red, and yellow fibres fusing together into a warm haze spreading across the sky, one incandescence which ignited the sky into a million atoms of stars, a breeze blows through her dark hair, as the volcano in the sky smolders through the night, ablazing the sea gold.

She got up and hung the lamp on the hook, she wrapped her shawl around herself before she got into the bedroom and slipped through the sheets.

Gently nestling her soul into the soft world of dreams.

Dreams soon wreathed into the morning wind, which spreads fresh smell through River's body, singing her cells alive as her eyes enfold to Sam's.

His green eyes glowed one leaf transparent and then another, however, they also had flecks of blue, blue as the birds' songs that ran together like interlacing of the mountain stream whose waters foam on the beach shore.

He smiled and said, "My sweet River, there is nirvana in your eyes, passion in your pulse, and white petals in your hair"

She moved her head slightly, there were indeed white petals flowing through her hair, she pulled Sam close and gently kissed his cheek.

She got up and slipped on a silk dress as they left the room.

    A few months pass after their vacation in Cannes, River and Sam had calmly lived in the nest of their own love in their home in London, until one night, Sam says to River,"I'm going to embark on a business trip in a foreign country" "for how long will you stay there, Sam?" "2 weeks or so" "Alright, but how will we keep in touch?", "Through email, of course" and so River helped Sam pack his bags that night and she bid him farewell at the airport. Many days pass, River began to feel cold on the inside even though it was warm on the flowers. So she began typing,

    -Dear Sam,
    I feel as if every day, the more we are apart, our heartstrings of communion slowly fade, as tendrils of you enbranch through my mind and enflame my memory, sweetly schorching through my veins, your eyes pierce through my ribcage and into my heart, unleashing the world horses of the night.
       -Love, River

    -Dear River,
    I am a slave to your memory, as my fingers touch the pillowcase, i feel the warmth of your body incinerating through the sheets that gradiate into blood red, like my lips, that expel sentences unquenched by the value of sound. But yet still burn through my skin, the flames crash the words you sent me, honeyed, like blood red of longing that soaks the sheets that make a slave to your memory.

        -Love, Sam

-Dear Sam,
A fervent, solemn passion wraps in a pure, powerful flame,
fusing you and me through the birth of a star, oh, Sam, there is
magic in your eyes, aligns the stars tesselate blooming the
cosmos petals from the center of the universe.
        -Love, River

-Dear River,
The center of my universe is you
        -Love, Sam

-Dear Sam,
Then why did i see a picture of you and that woman with your
arm around her in the newspaper? with the headline entitled,
"Married music producer turns into roguish playboy"
Sam, I lyed on the beach in Cannes, singing your song, the
waves remnants of you, vigourous strains as i begin to set my
wild heart free into plains of lust, my charred hooves begin the
enclave the fire round my heart strings, that were wound to
yours, and weaved back into another, sadness encurdles the
frozen glimmer in my eyes, so I pound on the hooves of
burning desire, and burst back into the fields.
        -Love? River

-Dear Sam,
My feet are on gravity, but it feels as if my heart could sink into
my glass eyes that stare at a mirror of reflection, cold through
its frozen glimmer, piercing rays of cruel affection, fury ablaze
ceases to dimmer, swimming in the seas of woe, the truth raptor
the heart of the thorns in its rose, sorrow caressing the wing of
the black crow, bursts the fires of the mirror's bang, through my
stained eyes of pain, shielded from the world's abundance, my
heart could sink in the abyss of burned tears, far from the sky's
sun dance.
        -Love? River

-Dear Sam,

I used to feel the warm heartbeat against my chest, your arms to envelope me into the soft glow of your eyes, color of the ocean, which flows down my cheeks into my heart, which you would used to touch with hands to dry my tears, and are embraced with soft lips, "do not worry" you would whisper, but my eyes open to the reality of the rain trickling down with the tears inside my heart.

-Love? River

The day that River wrote that final letter was the day she finally closed her laptop, before she heard a knocking on her door, It was Sam. His face looked torn, "River..." In immediance, she left his sight and walked away before he stopped her, "River, she was just my friend, please understand, we were just going to work together on an album, but nothing more." "GO, SAM!" tears rolling down her face as her glass of water crashed to the ground, the glass shattered with her heart to a million pieces, shining like stars and screaming, tears flaming like a phoenix as he lay with his knees on the floor, gripping her by the waist, the ocean burning through his face, "River, if i had cared for that woman, i would have not come back here, I saw in the depth of your eyes my own beauty reflected, River, you are a paradisal inferno scorching through my inner being, whatever i do with your cage, i cannot get at it, the savage, beautiful creature, it is you, River, it is the musk, the fragance of your soul that i desire." River's tears slowly began to dry as she began to realize, Sam had truly loved her, but love itself is like a thorned, scarlet rose. So she knelt down and held his face, he gently smiled "River..." he held her heart against his chest, River pressed her lips against his, the flames died out as the water evaporated into the mist that blanketed their love.

River lay on the couch, dissolved in the ethereal world of dreams as Sam held her in his arms and whispered "Breathe me...let your soul come with soft flight and nestle against my heart, breathe me through the warm honey spreading through my body, fire through my skin, rich, heavenly earth."

River gently awoke and whispered back "Sam, breathe me through the myriad of your aura that flows down through my heart like mountain water, leaves become branches in this wind that gently transports us the enclave of our love in the sun.

Sam whispered "River, flow through..." the writer's hands that stream through the enveloping of "Poetry Of The Soul", that will eternally bloom again in the eyes of the reader that embraces it as poetry embraces the soul.

Sacred

My sun kissed feet had walked through the lush greenery encircling the old grecian style floor of the Cyprian hotel, i entered the spa, which had looked surprisingly sleek and modern in comparision to the greek palace of the hotel, upon entering, gentle winds of peace had streamed through the sound of zen in our souls, the receptionists were kind and encouraged me to look at the brochure and decide what spa package i wanted, after deciding upon the "Simple Massage" package, i entered the massage room with the spa helpers, after preparation, i was laid on the massage bed, immersed through the warm almond oil that spread through the sound of zen that surrounded my being and rendered me floating in the bridge between unconsciousness and consciousness.

Warmth enveloped through the consciousness that evaporated into the mist that blanketed my body, i was numb, dissolved in the ethereal world of dreams as warmth held me in it's arms and whispered "breathe me...let your soul come with soft flight and nestle against my heart, breathe me through the warm oil spreading through your body, fire through your skin, rich, heavenly earth." The scent of the almond oil streaming through my nostrils as the sound of zen peripherated a realm far from the earth, humming sounds oscillated through the sound waves surrounding the invisible sea of sky as i flew while my body was still on the massage bed.

The spa worker's hands stroked my shoulders and through my neck, dark hair spilled on my skin as white petals floated from the sky, the zen music glowed one leaf transparent and then another through the zen music's birds' songs.

Calmness spilled through me as i closed my eyes and imagined the sunset, i would raise my lamp, its periphery glowing through the air flickering and flaming orange, red, and yellow fibres fusing together into a warm haze spreading across the sky, one incandescence which ignited the sky into a million atoms of stars, through her dark hair, as the volcano in the sky smolders through the night, ablazing the sea gold.

The zen music then shifts to the sounds of the rainforest, i close my eyes once again as rain trickles upon the leaves, i am immersed in the rainbow ribbons rippling through the reflecting light of hibiscus dew. I am lost in the rainforest, feeling the energy of the rising spirits of euphoria as i exhale and open my eyes, the spa worker tells me it is time to switch sides, i do, and the spa worker reapplies the warm almond oil and gently massages my consciousness, that is drifting in the sea of rose petals, the spa worker then continues, moving in circular motion like ripples on the water, circular like the moon, glowing through my being, that felt calm and happy. The wings of my soul opened, the golden aura of Nirvana flows through the zen, i close my eyes again as the spa worker massages my fingers, tousling them like the breeze swaying through the grass.

What felt most strange about the massage is that as i lay completely still and let myself under the warm blanket of zen, and even though i knew that the massage was a limited amount of time, i did not feel time, that flowed down like mountain water, breaking up rainbows into particles of blossom. I opened my eyes, like tiny Japanese fans, opening a dozen monarchs and swallowtails that flew into the sky, "Madamoiselle, you may prepare yourself, the massage session is complete"

The consciousness returned to its home and i arose, as if from a long, numbing sleep, i was supported from the massage bed and i patted myself dry with the towel as i walked out of the haven, or spa, i remember that day, that all the stress from my body had been washed away like a waterfall that bathed me in the cool reverie of calm. I could stop feeling that amazing experience until i reached our hotel room and cleaned myself in the shower, walking past the clear view of the Cyprian beach, i changed into my pajamas, the warm feeling still glowing through me.

The Endless River

For a long time in my life, feeling similiar to a loner, a loose string in the midst of my society's gossamer, consolating myself in the spreading green foliage of nature to conceal my burning waterfall, visceous of disconnection in a social gossamer of intricate connections, words and noise that surrounded my ears, I would walk through the streets, feeling alone, like no one would understand me. I felt spiritually empty and drained, i wish i could have said i was accepting of who i was, that i loved myself while the shadows of life haunt me and other people wanted to emotionally and spiritually hurt me, for i had suffered through many years of bullying in my youth and adolescence, that left me with a lasting feeling of weakness within myself. I told myself, i would never let them as i fell apart, through the years, everlasting tears fell down my face, my vision became a blur, everything began to flow down on me, I became the rain drops trickling down my cheek and into my soul. For a long time, i used to feel like i was of no value, a no one who would roam the grounds of the earth. And so, i decided that i was going to set myself free, dew drops trickle down the lights that glowed my true soul, a being of water, wearing the robes of waves as my dark hair flows in the waters that rose to meet the angel whom shone the fair light of the human's own inner beauty, i held a glass jar with the fountain of the sun inside, i raised it to the waters of the sea of clouds blazing the sea gold, the waves of time flew as they tears soon became the luminescence that streams upon the water, and from the water, bloomed the eternal white lotus, it's aura glows with the light of my awakening that beams clear from within my heart chakra, i close my eyes, i was forever healed as the shadows dissolved and i drifted from consciousness and into the unveiling gates of dawn, floating within the endless river, the eternal spiritual odyssey of the soul.

Water

I close my eyes, I have heard the river flowing silk through my veins,
I have heard the crystal shower through my hair, I have heard the
waves on my skin, the world becomes the ocean, I become the water,
and the water becomes me, and the sea of spirits that glow within the
ocean of our eyes shining the transparent calligraphy of waves, waters
of Inner zen, flowing through the journey within, the odyssey of the
soul within, I swim into a realm where beautiful souls speak in a
language of electromagnetic molecules that vibrate and dance,
different auras of the spectrum collide, melting magnetic attraction,
dissolving in the waves surrounding silhouettes swimming in the deep
waters and letting their presences flow over me, as we aimlessly
became the mist swaying at the regions where sound never reaches,
where the light touches the slow dance of spirits in communion with
the infinite sea of love within, within the ocean of wisdom that dwells
in the one heart of the humanity.

Tree Of Life

In the dreams beyond the sea of glowing white,
where humans would listen to a soul singer, similar to
myself, ascending her voice to the heavens, showering the
realms with transcendental, etheric feeling glowing from within the
eyes of youth similar to the young men Nicholas and James, whom
entered a woman's home and she was greeted by the siblings as James
proclaimed, "will you tell us another one of your stories?" "of course,
James" as she smiled and sat down with her blanketed thick chair,
"both of you take your seats" as Nicholas and James took their
wooden chairs and sat down to listen. "In a realm wreathed within the
cosmos, there was a green paradise where the tree of life resides, in
the tree of life, there lived cocoons, inside those cocoons were
luminescent golden seeds that developed into the beings of the
universe, the humans that possessed wisdom and knowledge higher
than the ones on earth, would eventually be born, after their birth they
would be taken by large beautiful butterflies of different colors and
species, and the other beings were taken by their own species, the
humans were nourished and fed by the women of the town, and their
learning was nurtured by both the women and the men of that town,
one day, there was a seed that was nurturing the growth of a girl"
"what was the name of the girl?" James asked "at first, James, they
have no names, because they are first spirits that are created by God,
and those spirits live inside the seeds that are united by the tree" "how
does this tree survive?" Nicholas asks "It survives by the power of
love" she replied, "how does it slowly die?" James asked, "when love
fades in humanity and the blade of war is unsheathed and sheds the
blood of the innocent" "continue the story of the girl" Nicholas said as
she continued "ah yes, the girl, when she was born, the leaders of the
town later gave her the name Celesta, a beautiful girl with translucent
skin and hair and eyes as dark as the night, they shine as bright as the
stars within her." "was there ever a time when the tree was dying?"
James asked, "In the Great War, it was" she replies, "when the leaders
of the town and their economic interests clashed with the interests of
an alien species, they fought to death until Celesta involved herself
and saved the tree of life from death, "how?" Nicholas asked, "when
Celesta became a grown woman, she had fallen in love with a man, a

human man who was sent by the alien species to kill her, he was was chasing her until she fell inside the open door of the tree, there, the embers of the tree glowed alive, whispering the universal language of the heart, love, Celesta stopped the man and held his hand and whispered, "the essence of darkness is light" and so the man was changed to a being of good, and the tree of life bloomed back it's leaves and flowers and the barren wasteland of war grew back into its former lush green, the animals eventually returned, and peace was returned to the land" Nicholas then claims "wait, but what about the war between the alien species and the leaders?" she then replies "the tree of life blooms every spirit in the universe, because of love, the beings of the universe turn to war when there is no love, when the tree of life was revived, so was love in the hearts of the beings of the universe, and thus, peace was fully restored." "Thank you for your story" James said, "I agree, I liked it" Nicholas chimed in, before Nicholas then said, "Is there any chance, that you might be Celesta" she then smiled as she arose from the chair in her flowing white dress, "Follow me, Nicholas and James" she said as Nicholas and James followed her out of the cabin and into the long, green fields, "take my hand" she says as Nicholas and James take both of her hands and they fly from the sky, "wait, but how will we breathe in space?" "My magic will help you, for I am Celesta" as the embers flowed through their skin as they flew into the sea of stars.

Letter

As she read the words with her dark rimmed glasses, clear lenses that
reflected the rainbow spectrum within her eyes, her heart glowing
with with the words of love and peace that she wrote, a spiritual letter
to the foreign fields, where she felt free, in a loose, fair dress as she
danced, she danced freely as the pan-pipes began to play and she felt
the music of peace as the flower petals were swaying around her
flowing hair, she laid herself in the grass, she then imagined, as she
lay in the fields of peace, how war was like, she began by writing
about a soldier in the war, "A warm, gentle breeze then blew after
dark, very refreshing despite the sharpness of the war atmosphere that
often struck deep into your heart like a knife, seeping into a scarlet
soil not worth dying for. I closed my eyes, lifted my head and took a
deep breath. I sniffed the soil, decaying vegetation and pungent leaf
mold that smelled like the bloodied, dead bodies of the innocence.
The night was our friend now and as well as our enemy. Having never
smoked, I was more sensitive to odors than most, Sound carries well
in the jungle, with my vision impaired by darkness, it would be my
hearing and sense of smell that would alert me to the presence of
intruders, only alert, and not prevent me from the power of death. In
the blur of the distance, The faint barking of a solitary animal in the
distance suddenly broke the silence. It was probably only the barking
deer that lived in the forests, a short time later, I heard several more

animals, a little closer this time. I realized that the sound was dogs' barking. The moon was up now, with a blood red tinge. I reached out and grabbed the shoulder of my soldier companion, Bell, gently but firmly. Leaning over slowly, I whispered that we were going to have company before long. Those dogs barking in the distance meant that men were up and moving around in some nearby village or encampment. I assumed that all the dogs in the neighbourhood barking as they were doing now meant that a lot of people were up and moving. Maybe they were made nervous by the sound of our helicopter in the area earlier, what ever it was that had alerted them would cause them to search the area before much longer. Later in the night, we again heard the faint thuds of opposition walking the trail between us and the clearing. They began randomly firing rounds into the surrounding jungle, They were close enough that we could see the muzzle flashes of their weapons. Bell leaned close and whispered. "They're trying to make us give away our position", "We would be foolish to". I replied, with my mouth was dry as the desert, and my hands were soaking in sweat that should have satisfied my thirst. Fearing dehydration, I swallowed a couple of salt tablets, and drank a little water from my canteen. There would be no time to do so later. My heart picked up a pace as the adrenaline began to surge through my system. It was time to move. my soldier comrade, Bell followed me in a crouch, his eyes at a level a little above mine. I stopped every few meters to watch and listen for sounds from the enemy, there was no sound: no insects, no birds, nothing. Even the wind had calmed, There was no movement among the trees and brush around us. It was as if the jungle itself was watching, waiting, it was waiting for my

Death. We made a very little noise, but each crackle of a dead leaf, each snap of a twig, echoed through our minds like a cannon shot. I began to breathe in short, rapid gasps, nostrils flaring. Then I smelled something different, It was the odour of our sweat, of clothes saturated with our lives. The opposition were hidden around the base of three abandoned anthills rising from the forest floor. We were already face down in the dirt. I felt and heard a rushing sound that surged through my heartbeat. The sound of guns exploded, the death of the innocent, there was little cover between the enemy shadows and us. To stay meant death. Yet, as we ran deeper into the forest, I expected every step to be my last. I saw Bell, running in front of everyone, stagger as his rucksack blew up on his back. An enemy had hit him centre-mass. He stumbled momentarily, then was up and running again. The contents of his pack had stopped the bullet. I saw something move and then blend into the dark shadows. Then I spotted him. It appeared to be a part of the enemy that was closing in on us. The enemy was gliding from tree to tree. I saw one…two…three small, dark forms moving nearer and nearer. Enemy fire enflamed through the red sky as the heavy whopping of rotor blades of an approaching Helicopter came in fast as I heard the roar of the gunships firing, I lifted my head and saw the two Helicopters hovering just above the far tree line, covering the rest of the team as they broke cover and ran for the pickup Helicopter. I looked up as Bell ran past me screaming, "Are you coming McHale?" I was up and running as we piled aboard as the gunships fired into the forest. The Helicopter lifted, dipped toward the forest as it picked up forward speed, then rose above the trees and the moon had set, and the darkest hour of the night had come and gone, the spirits of the innocence rose from the ashes of war and into the foreign fields of the afterlife". As she wrote that last sentence, burning tears began to flow and trickle down her face, when will the innocence be mercied from the blades of tyranny? the blades of war? she then rose from the fields as the light of peace manifested itself in the predawn light of the Phoenix rise from the east of the fields.

The Philosopher

Reader, in a quiet street in London, there had rumors of a woman named "The Philosopher", people would come and ask her questions, she did have one rule, she was not a psychologist who dealt with personal issues. But rather, she would her share merely her perspective and ideas from people who ask her question. Because it was a quiet street, not many came, except for today, when we will tell the tale of a young British man named James, who had come to visit "The Philosopher", he knocked on the door and a woman had opened the door, "Hello James, welcome, come on inside" and so they entered into a warm, welcoming quiet room with shelves of books. "So James, tell me what you have come to ask me." "I will begin by asking, even though my mates don't understand why i decided to come here, even though they know i greatly fancy rumors. Why do you live such a quiet life?"

"Sometimes, having your own quality time, James, lets you close your eyes and wander through the warm, lush garden of eden."

"Tell me about thoughts and the human mind"

"Thoughts, James, flow through your mind like koi fish in clearwater, which is your mind"

"What is your idea of physical beauty in a man?"

"I would rather kiss a beautiful soul, rather than judging purely upon a handsome face"

"What makes a man, a true man and a true leader, what is maturity to you?"

"What makes a true man is based upon the eyes of the beholder and their perspective, however, you ask my opinion, and i believe that a chauvinistic man is no true man, a true man is one who is untainted by power, for to truly test a man, you must give him power, a true leader is a man who follows good and acts good, however, if he calls himself leader, he is no true leader".

She took a long, deep breath, and continued, "Maturity, James, I find to be a very interesting thing, lets give an example of you in the workplace, you can be hardworking, and strong, and that would allow a good example and impression on your work peers and your employer or boss, but will that determine the maturity in your actions, behavior, and, finally, the knowledge in your mind shown outside of the workplace or social area? when your true colours show behind garments and garments of facade?"

" I don't think that it will truly determine, hey, I thought i was the one asking you the questions?" he said with a smile

"Of course" as she smiled back, "continue, James"

 "What do you think of the young generation, as in children? and teaching in schools?"

"The young generation is a treasure, and that treasure must not be tainted by an undeveloped, authoritarian type of school, where the young are caged birds, greatly yearning to sing their inner beauty, they ruffle their silk of colours of creativity in a prison, where they sadly grow up in. And, i know its unrelated, but sometimes, i wonder if women and men live in the greatest, most terrible cages, which is, themselves."

She then continued, "I will never quite understand why schools teach children to be too rational, assuming everything in the world is backed up by facts, the minds of children are eventually built up with facts of science, we are exploding cavilcades of iridescent creativity, passions and emotions and tongues of fire, the beings of the universe are magical, beautiful creations of God and so are we."

"Interesting idea, tell me about the quality of words versus the quantity of words"

"Good question, James, let us take the example of you, you are speaking on stage to a crowd, and now, let us take the length of a rope and the rope itself, you want to hold something with the rope like you want to hold the crowd with your words. Now, there is a difference between the length of the rope and the fabric of its support. Length of words, like the length of the rope, do not truly determine the fabric of its support, which is validity of action or validity in general, length of words do not truly determine truth. The quantity of words does not determine the quality of words".

"But, maybe sometimes, for example, when in love, words do not matter and it is only hearts that speak?"

The philosopher smiled, "Sometimes, when the hearts speak to each other, the physical world around them dissolves, and they become they become like those koi fishes we spoke about earlier, however, this time, they are swimming in their own clear water."

"Tell me about people and first impressions"

"People must not solely rely upon first impressions, the first impressions will not reveal all of the true self of that human, I think the best solution Is to truly get to know the human before acting wisely."

"In accordance to a relationship between two people, what is the difference between desire and love?"

"You ask my opinion of the difference between desire and love, desire is a only a physical attraction, but love is the collision of two spirits, the merging of spiritual light and passionate fire"

"Tell me what is peace for you?"

"Peace, for me, Is resting near the sun, and the quiet images of breath merge with the crystalline aura glowing through the waters of consciousness" she then continued, "peace is seeing the diamond water flowing down the stream, seeing a flower blossoming the birth of the star, peace is when I discovered the meaning of life, to love, to love nature, to love and appreciate myself, however, at the same time, being cautious not to extend self-love to the point of narcissism"

"Tell me, what is Zen?"

"Zen, James, is the balance between body and mind, like the wind balancing the gentle curves of a bird's wings"

"Tell me how does a flower relates to the inner beauty in humans?"

"The simplicity of the stem, brings forth the delicate flowers within"

"What is the origin of humans?"

"The origin is Love"

"And what about War?"

"Love will conquer War, in all of its forms"

"You speak of forms, what about Matter?"

"Matter is what we are before are created in the womb, and what we will become when we pass away, so essentially, Matter is the beginning and end".

"What about Time?"

"Imagine, James, in a kaleidescope of heartbeats, through them, the waves of time crash on the shore of stars, through the eyes of humanity"

"Tell me who you are, and what do you see"

"I will tell you who I am, James, am the trees, mountains, waves, endless fjords, rivers, oceans, and fields of daisies, I could be a snake and I could be a butterfly, floating on the surfaces of the fields of white roses, the petals float in the wind, I am now that lone petal floating in the blue sky, I unite with the ground and I am reborn as another rose that is met by a bee, I now see through the molecular eyes of the bee and return to the hive that drips the rich, viscous golden liquid of honey, I fly out of the hive and shapeshift into a dove, a delicate, powerful symbol of hope in the midst of war, I am now the soldier, a woman who, on the exterior, is a virtous representation of courage, bravery, and strength, when in truth, I am a woman who could possibly be struggling with my own inner wars, and I know that as a soldier in life, that life can be a double edged sword, a sword, In this case, represents any weapon and can be used to strike down nature or nourish and help the growth of the earth, I see through the eyes of humans throughout history who have searched for the poetry of the soul, when the poetry of the soul is within them, I have seen prime ministers, monarchs, presidents who have held the sword that can shine good, powerful leadership, or be the accursed sword of terror that drips the blood of innocent civilians. I see through the eyes of a child, an angel shines through its eyes, smiling so freely and brightly, like the launch of a multi-coloured parrot through the blue sky, I am now that parrot, a flurry of silken colours in my flight through the surround sounds of the rainforest, I am the lone dew that drops into the soil and blooms back again as a white rose of the endless snow white fields, where the innocent spirits of civilians float away from the bloodied sword of war"

James, for a long amount of minutes, could not say anything, before he said,

"You are truly fascinating as they say, but, as much i would love to stay, I must leave now because I am late for my lunch appointment"

"I understand," as she smiled, "have a pleasant lunch and lovely day, James"

And so James walked through the hallways and out the main door, he drove out the quiet street, her words remaining forever in his memory, as she returned to her haven of knowledge, the haven of infinity.

The Call Within

I sat at my table with my cup of coffee, warmth of a robust, earthy,
rich aroma enveloping my tastebuds, lingering on chocolate
undertones, laced with sensuous caramel. I then began to write, "Dear
Spirit, I know that you see through my eyes, unconscious interpreter,
but my physical self feels so tired and exhausted with all the shadows
of burdens that surround me, every day, I feel alone, unloved,
unwanted, like a feather floating through space, a flower in a
firestorm, the water floods me and I feel like I cannot escape the
tsunami, the tsunami of people rushing past me and rushing through
me, mending or breaking, healing or hurting, I feel like I am sinking
through an endless abyss, far from the reach of the sun, the moon and
the stars"

The warm, night wind blows through the curtains of my windows, it
whispers to me, "the break of dawn comes from within, only you can
hold back the rivers of the tsunami by achieving the balance with the
waters of your inner self, and once you feel at peace with yourself,
others will not affect you, perhaps they will mirror your peace, and
feel at peace with themselves, let the water flow, it flows like the
shine of the sun, the moon, and the stars upon your skin, and once you
achieve peace with them, the balance of light and dark, you will rise,
your body of you is a glowing phoenix of the cosmos, you will sing
the orb of earth, the trees, the animals, and the clouds, starbeams soft

in love's delicate rain that touches the night tapestry of an illumined sea, the interlunar dreams of you clear through a dusk aery veil, the sun rushes under before it rises in the morning, white robe of ethereal pearl, that is you, human" I then felt these words and smiled, I went down from the house and walked through the fields until I found him, sitting by the white light above, touched by Indigo night, under the soft and sweet eclipse of the meeting of our two eyes, soul meets soul on lovers' lips, the night is calm, out of the stream of sound, a violet gazes upon the moon, the universe is silent as our spirits collide.

Mystic

If you ever wish to find me, come find me when I am seated in a crowded place in solitude, I will never truly fit in this hive, perhaps I was never really supposed to fit in, poets and stargazers are a beautiful colourful collision, but you never even have to be a poet by words, In fact, you are already are a poet in your own way, for humans are beings of expression, I have always loved my soul divine, my heart free and wild, thoughts like fish going upstream, like wild flowers of the universe, humans, we must bloom wherever we go, only we can free ourselves and love ourselves and our surroundings quite wholeheartingly, to embrace and love the world with passion and be beautiful minds in a world of grey, cosmic cavilcades that find love and peace with themselves, our bodies are only vessels that hold the beauty within, to have the colourful gypsy dreams, the souls of wanderers in the Garden Of Eden surrounding us, the listeners within the eyes that narrate tales of the universe, If you ever wish to see me, I will be in the river of dreams, perhaps drinking Rose syrup drink and singing along with the beautiful minds full of dreams, colours, and exploding stars in the cosmic clusters.

Venus

I am Venus, rising from the sea, silhouettes in the waves of light, in the sea of transcendence to a higher dimension, crashing waves in the cosmos, the endless depths, my vivid, soft watercolour wings of my spirit, love light glowing, living, breathing within my indigo soul. A soft wind tousles the flowers that fly through my dark hair as i close my eyes and become the eternal spirit of love that has roamed the earth for thousands of years. I saw through the eyes of my soul the birth of the first star, that bloomed the first flower from the earth, i saw the evolution of man that walked this earth and breathes the same air as the birds, whom melodically chime their celestial songs among the leaves as they fly so elegantly and gracefully, before perching on branches in the tree of life, singing the language of love my spirit knew and felt so well. Solar wind flowing through my dress as i see the sky of earth, enshrouded by snow white painted clouds on the earth, an orb of light in the many universes within the humans, the tapestry like the cells within my moonlight skin, that touches the earth, and embraces the heavenly plants and animals, as well the humans of peace and love, i place the scent of a flower to my nose, the rich, flavorful and strong scent of one of many flora i held so dearly, the lotus.

Water

-

I close my eyes, I have heard the river flowing silk through my veins,
I have heard the crystal shower through my hair, I have heard the
waves on my skin, the world becomes the ocean, I become the water,
and the water becomes me, and the sea of spirits that glow within the
ocean of our eyes shining the transparent calligraphy of waves, waters
of Inner zen. Flowing through the journey within, the odyssey of the
soul within, I swim into a realm where beautiful souls speak in a
language of electromagnetic molecules that vibrate and dance,
different auras of the spectrum collide, melting magnetic attraction,
dissolving in the waves surrounding silhouettes swimming in the deep
waters and letting their presences flow over me, as we aimlessly
became the mist swaying at the regions where sound never reaches,
where the light touches the slow dance of spirits in communion with
the infinite sea of love within, within the ocean of wisdom that dwells
in the one heart of the humanity.

Printed in the United States of America

First Printing, 2016

Lulu Press, Inc.

ISBN: 978-1-365-07814-9

Beirut, Lebanon

Artwork:
www.etsy.com/shop/8Visions8

ISBN 978-1-365-07814-9

90000

9 781365 078149

Lightning Source UK Ltd.
Milton Keynes UK
UKOW03n2124090517

300829UK00003B/52/P